ISAAC ASIMOV'S
Library of the Universe

Did
Comets
Kill the
Dinosaurs?

by Isaac Asimov

Gareth Stevens
London • Milwaukee

Grateful thanks to **Professor Martin Greenberg** for his abundant energy, technical skill, and personal commitment to this project.

The reproduction rights to all photographs and illustrations in this book are controlled by the individuals or institutions credited on page 32 and may not be reproduced without their permission.

A Gareth Stevens Children's Books edition. Edited, designed, and produced by

Gareth Stevens, Inc.

7317 West Green Tree Road   Milwaukee, Wisconsin 53223, USA

Text copyright © 1988 by Nightfall, Inc.
End matter copyright © 1988 by Gareth Stevens, Inc.
Format copyright © 1988 by Gareth Stevens, Inc.

ISBN 0-8368-7027-1
First published in the United States and Canada by Gareth Stevens, Inc.
First published in the United Kingdom in 1988 by Gareth Stevens Children's Books

Cover art © Julian Baum

Designer: Laurie Shock
Picture research: Kathy Keller
Artwork commissioning: Kathy Keller and Laurie Shock
Project editors: Mark Sachner & MaryLee Knowlton

Technical adviser and consulting editor: Greg Walz-Chojnacki

1 2 3 4 5 6 7 8 9 93 92 91 90 89 88

CONTENTS

Introduction

The Universe is an enormously large place in which human beings live. It's only in the last 50 years or so that we've found out how large it really is.

It's only natural that we should want to understand the place in which we live, and in the last 50 years we have developed new instruments to help us learn more about our vast home. We have radio telescopes, satellites, probes, and many other things that have told us far more about the Universe than could possibly have been imagined when I was young.

Nowadays, we have seen planets up close. We have learned about quasars and pulsars, about black holes and supernovas. We have learned amazing facts about how the Universe may have come into being and how it may end. Nothing can be more astonishing and more interesting.

Facts about the Universe aren't always about the faraway. Right here on Earth, there were once giant animals called dinosaurs. About 65 million years ago, they disappeared. The reason why they vanished might be found in outer space. Out there we may discover not only the secret of the dinosaur's end, but also fantastic dangers that could threaten our Earth in the future, and threaten us as well.

And it may be that by learning about space, we will be able to escape those dangers. I'll tell you about it in this book.

If we had lived in Montana, USA, when Tyrannosaurus did, he could have swallowed us whole.

Rudolf Zallinger/Peabody

Giants of the Earth

Once, millions of years ago, large animals called dinosaurs walked on Earth. Some of them were up to 27.4 m (90 feet) long. Others may have weighed as much as 91 tonnes (100 tons) or more — equal to about 12 large elephants!

The largest dinosaurs were plant-eaters, but the picture you see here is of a meat-eater, the most terrifying that ever lived. It is a tyrannosaur. It was nearly 15.2 m (50 feet) long and was heavier than most elephants. Its head was up to 1.5 m (5 feet) long, and its teeth could be over 17.8 cm (7 inches) long. It was not something you would want to meet!

Were some dinosaurs warm-blooded?

The dinosaurs were reptiles. We can tell that from the structure of their bones. All the reptiles that are alive now — turtles, lizards, snakes, alligators — are cold-blooded. This means that when the weather is cold, they're cold, too, and become very sluggish and slow in their movements. Some scientists are sure that some dinosaurs were quite active. These scientists wonder whether some of the dinosaurs were warm-blooded. After all, birds and mammals are descended from reptiles, and they are warm-blooded. When did that start? So far, there is no way to tell.

The Mystery of the Dinosaurs

The dinosaurs first evolved about 225 million years ago. For 140 million years, they ruled the Earth. Some kinds died out, but others came into being. Then, around 65 million years ago, they <u>all</u> died out. All we have left, now, are bones, teeth, footprints, and other fossils, or evidence of prehistoric life.

Why did dinosaurs die? Scientists have wondered if the climate changed, if small animals took to eating dinosaur eggs, or if a nearby exploding star showered Earth with deadly x-rays. No explanation seemed quite right.

© Diane Gabriel/Milwaukee Public Museum

The size and depth of a footprint can help scientists know how much a dinosaur weighed.

Not all fossils are underfoot. These fossils are in the wall, once underground, of a quarry in Colorado, USA.

Ultraheavy . . . ultralong . . . ultratall: it's Ultrasaurus!

The largest known land animal of all time was a dinosaur called Ultrasaurus. The few bones discovered so far tell scientists that the animal must have weighed 91-127 tonnes (100-140 tons) and measured 30-35 m (100-115 feet) long and about 17 m (56 feet) tall — about three times as tall as a giraffe. This means it would have been as tall as a five-storey house.

Death from Space?

In 1978, scientists found some rare materials called iridium in rocks that were about 65 million years old. There was more iridium in these rocks than in others, and it came just when the dinosaurs died. Where did it come from? Possibly from outer space. Meteoroids are rocks that move through space and sometimes collide with Earth. We often see them enter Earth's atmosphere as fiery meteors. Meteoroids that strike Earth's surface are called meteorites. Some meteorites are quite large. In Arizona, USA, there is a hole, or crater, gouged out by a large meteorite. Some craters are so old they've worn away, but scientists can detect signs of those craters from the air.

The Barringer Meteor Crater in Arizona, USA, is about 1.2 km (3/4 mile) across. Scientists think it was created by a meteorite impact 50,000 years ago.

One of the world's most beautiful craters is in western Australia. It is called the Wolf Creek Crater.

Global Winter

Could something striking Earth 65 million years ago have killed the dinosaurs? It could be so. If the object was big enough, it could have gouged out a huge quantity of rock and soil, ground it into dust, and flung that dust high in the air for miles and miles.

The dust would have spread out all over Earth. It would have blocked the sunlight. Little light or heat would have reached Earth for months, or even years. The plants would have died, and then large animals that ate plants or other animals would have died. Smaller animals might have nibbled at bark or seeds, or eaten the frozen bodies of larger animals. Some of them would have survived. But the dinosaurs would be gone.

Global winter: With dust blocking the Sun's heat and light, Earth would be cold and dark. Most plants and animals would die.

Earth-crossers: Some comets and asteroids travel dangerously close to Earth. In this picture, the paths of the comets are shown in yellow, and the paths of stray asteroids are in red.

Earth Under Fire

Are there large objects in space that can hit Earth? Yes. Scientists have detected objects 1.6 km (1 mile) or more across that can come within a few million kilometres of Earth. A few dozen of these have been detected, but there are probably others we just haven't seen. There may be more than a thousand in all. None of them comes close enough to hit us, but the gravitational pull of planets can change their paths.

Some day, one of these objects, on a changed path, might crash into us — just as one might have crashed into Earth 65 million years ago!

© Julian Baum (series of four)

© Mark Paternostro

Lured by Earth's gravitational pull, a meteoroid approaches our prehistoric world (1) and enters the atmosphere as a fiery meteor (2). Now a meteorite, it collides with Earth (3) as a dinosaur watches (4). Will this mean the end of his food supply?

1

2

3

4

Asteroid or Comet?

Some of these nearby objects are made of rock or metal. We call these objects asteroids. Others are made up mostly of ice, and we call these comets. If a comet were to hit Earth, it would speed through the air and heat up. The ice would vaporize to gas and expand in a loud explosion. It might not reach the ground and leave a crater, but it would do much damage.

An icy comet vaporizes as it speeds toward Earth. Its target: Siberia.

Leonid Kulik/Smithsonian

ГОРА „ОБЕДЕННАЯ" ВИД НА СЕВЕРО-ВОСТОК.

Сплошной ориентированный бурелом в 10-15 км от центральной площади.

Siberia, site of a possible comet strike in 1908 near the Tunguska River. Leonid Kulik, a Soviet scientist, investigated the blast in 1927. He described the area in this picture, dated 24 February 1929. The words are written in Russian, as you can see.

In 1908, something struck the middle of Siberia. It knocked down every tree in an area more than 18 km (11 miles) across. But it didn't kill anyone, because no one was living there. Some scientists believe the object was a small comet that exploded in the atmosphere before it could hit Earth.

15

Comets are made of lighter material than asteroids are. If a comet is large enough, however, it can do as much damage as any asteroid.

The object that may have hit Earth 65 million years ago didn't seem to leave a crater, so scientists thought it might have been a comet.

Of course, the object might have hit the ocean, and the crater might be at the bottom of the sea! In 1987, a huge crater was found in the sea bottom near Nova Scotia, in Canada. It is 45 km (28 miles) across, and perhaps it is what is left of a possible collision that may have killed the dinosaurs.

© Julian Baum

Comets — a sign of doom?

In older times, before people knew what comets were, they thought comets were warnings from the heavens telling of a coming disaster. When comets appeared in the sky, people were terrified. And sure enough, whenever a comet appeared something terrible would happen. A war would come, a plague would rage, or the king would die, or something. Of course, even when a comet didn't appear terrible things like that also happened. Somehow people never seemed to notice that.

The Nova Scotia crater as it might look deep beneath the sea: Could this be all that remains of what killed the dinosaurs?

Where Do Comets Come From?

If a comet is large enough, it might survive being heated by the air and gouge out a crater on land or under the sea. Some scientists think it was a comet, not an asteroid, that killed the dinosaurs. A Dutch astronomer, Jan Oort, believed that there are many billions of comets slowly orbiting the Sun many times farther away than the planets. This 'Oort cloud' might be where Earth-colliders start.

Comets in the Oort cloud: The gravity of passing stars may pull these comets out of the Oort cloud and into Earth's orbit.

Comets — a look back in time?

The Sun and the planets probably formed out of an original cloud of dust and gas. We can't be sure what the original cloud was made of. In the billions of years the Solar system has existed, the Sun and the planets have changed a lot. On Earth, for instance, some of the original matter was lost to space, and some sank to the centre. Scientists think comets are samples of the original cloud that have not changed with the years. That is one reason why they were so excited when spacecraft passed near Halley's Comet in 1986. It was the first time a comet was studied up close. Further studies on comets may tell us more about the beginnings of the Earth.

What Makes Showers?

Some scientists think that every 26 million years comets from the Oort cloud hit the Earth and cause different kinds of life forms to die out. It isn't hard to imagine a large comet striking Earth accidentally, but what could cause collisions to occur like clockwork every 26 million years?

One thought is that perhaps the Sun has a small, dark companion star that circles it once every 26 million years. This star has been named 'Nemesis'. At one end of its path, this little companion could enter the Oort cloud. Its gravitational pull would send billions of comets into our part of the Solar system. Some of those comets could hit Earth.

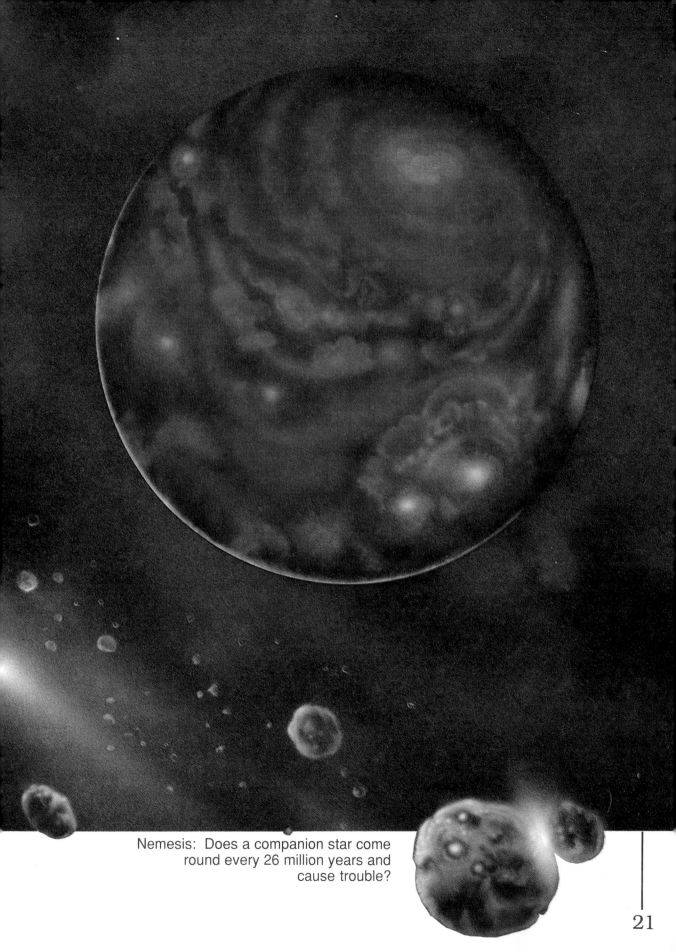

Nemesis: Does a companion star come
round every 26 million years and
cause trouble?

Orbiting the Galaxy

Nemesis is not the only possible explanation for regular collisions between Earth and comets. After all, Nemesis has never been seen, and we don't know for sure if it even exists. But we do know that the Sun travels about the centre of our Galaxy, carrying Earth and all the planets and comets with it.

ESO

The Sombrero Galaxy: a star's wavy course across the galactic midline. Our Sun follows a wavy course that takes it above and below the galactic midline of the Milky Way, crossing the plane roughly every 33 million years.

The Sun follows a slightly wavy path, first above the midline of the Galaxy, then below it, then above it again, and so on. Every time it passes through the midline, where there are more stars and dust clouds, a stronger gravitational pull may send the comets into our neighbourhood.

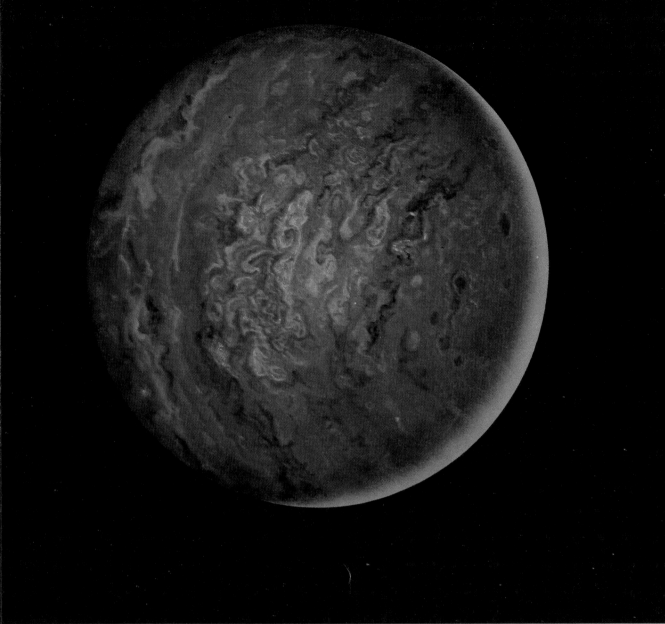

An Unknown Planet?

The Sun's passing through our Galaxy's midline may not explain these collisions, either. Some astronomers think the cause may be a distant planet we haven't detected yet. Perhaps when this planet is at the far end of its path around the Sun, it reaches the inner edge of the Oort cloud.

It would reach the far end of its path every few thousand years, but the orbit might wobble so that the far end would be above the Oort cloud or below it most of the time. Every 26 million years it would go through the cloud and send comets flying in our direction.

Planet X: Does a still unknown planet of the Solar system bump into the Oort cloud every 26 million years and send comets and asteroids to Earth? If so, such a planet would be so distant and faint that it would be hard to detect.

© Michael Carroll

Welcome back, stranger!

Sometimes, we may think a kind of animal is no longer alive, but then it surprises us. There is a fish called a coelacanth which was believed to have died out along with the dinosaurs 65 million years ago. In 1938, a ship near South Africa caught a fish in its net that turned out to be a coelacanth. Since then over a dozen coelacanths have been caught. The coelacanth did not die out, but it lives in deep water and usually stays out of human sight.

Are there dinosaurs among us today?

Mammals are descended from certain early reptiles that were <u>not</u> dinosaurs. But birds may be descended from reptiles that <u>were</u> dinosaurs. Some scientists think that birds are still much like little dinosaurs which have grown feathers and become warm-blooded. So is it fair to say that dinosaurs have all vanished? Might we say that some of them sit in trees and sing? Scientists haven't made up their minds.

What's in Store for Earth?

We're about halfway between major comet strikes, if the theory of collisions every 26 million years is correct. We might be hit at any time, of course, but the real danger may not come for another 13 million years.

Will that be the end of human beings? Maybe not. By that time, we should have settlements on various bodies of the Solar system and we should have built cities in space.

We could be watching for the approach of any dangerous body. We could push it aside, or even destroy it, by using advanced science. Then we'd be sure that no collision from outer space could kill <u>us</u> the way it killed the dinosaurs.

If the comets are coming in just 13 million years, maybe we should plan to be out when they arrive. NASA scientists and engineers have designed permanent colonies. These colonies could be on other planets, such as Mars, or in space itself. This one looks like a giant wheel in space. A large mirror directs sunlight into the colony.

NASA

NASA

Space colony: home for 10,000 people 402,000 km (250,000 miles) from Earth. This space colony would be constructed of ore mined from the Moon.

NASA

This proposed space colony has a bridge like the Golden Gate Bridge in San Francisco, California, USA. The colony would be a cylinder 30.6 km (19 miles) long and 6.4 km (4 miles) in diameter. In this picture, city lights are reflected in the large mirrored panels that direct sunlight into the colony.

Fact File: Did Comets Kill the Dinosaurs?

Why Did the Dinosaurs and Other Prehistoric Reptiles Die Out?

POSSIBLE CAUSES	POSSIBLE EFFECTS
Changes in climate	Some types of plants disappeared, leaving some dinosaurs without food
Small animals eating dinosaur eggs	Fewer dinosaurs reaching adulthood and reproducing
Major catastrophes or natural disruptions on Earth - such as the rise of mountain chains, huge floods, or volcanic eruptions	Sudden death of plant and animal life

The Age of Reptiles

Here is a pictorial walk back through prehistory. Our walk begins at the left, with the time 65 million years ago. This is when dinosaurs disappeared from the face of the Earth. Our walk ends at the far right, some 400 million years ago, before the Age of Reptiles began. Dots above the names will help you find the animals in the picture.

CRETACEOUS PERIOD   **JURASSIC PERIOD**

65
Millions of Years Ago   135

Triceratops   Pteranodon   Anatosaurus   Rhamphorhynchus   Allosauru

Triceratops   Tyrannosaurus   Apatosaurus (Brontosaurus)   Stegosaurus

Ankylosaurus   Archaeopteryx

Archaeopter

Why Did the Dinosaurs and Other Prehistoric Reptiles Die Out?

POSSIBLE CAUSES	POSSIBLE EFFECTS
An asteroid or a very large meteorite striking the Earth	Dust thrown out from the impact blocking out light and heat from the Sun for months or years, killing plants and causing large animals that ate plants to die, too
Comet strike or shower	Life-forms die out, kinds and numbers depending on how much damage done by comet
A nearby star exploding	Earth showered with deadly X-rays

Rudolf Zallinger/Peabody

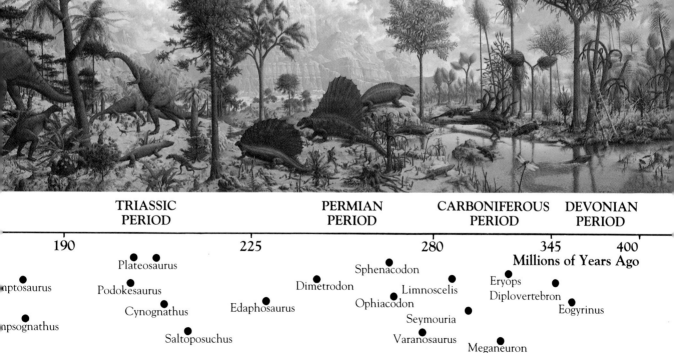

TRIASSIC PERIOD		PERMIAN PERIOD	CARBONIFEROUS PERIOD	DEVONIAN PERIOD

190   225   280   345   400
Millions of Years Ago

Plateosaurus
Sphenacodon
...ptosaurus
Eryops
Podokesaurus
Dimetrodon
Limnoscelis
Diplovertebron
Cynognathus
Edaphosaurus
Ophiacodon
Eogyrinus
...psognathus
Seymouria
Saltoposuchus
Varanosaurus
Meganeuron

More Books About Comets and the Dinosaurs

Here are more books about comets and dinosaurs. If you are interested in them, check your library or bookshop.

Comets. Hamer (Franklin Watts)
Comets and Meteors. Couper (Franklin Watts)
Dinosaurs. McCord (Usborne)
How the Dinosaurs Became Extinct. Fernando (Merlin Books)
How We Found Out About Comets. Asimov (Longman)
How We Found Out About Dinosaurs. Asimov (Longman)
The New Dinosaur Library. (series of 4). Burton/Dixon (Gareth Stevens)
A New Look at the Dinosaurs. Charig (Facts on File)

Places to Visit

Comets and Other Cosmic Treats
You can explore the Universe — including the places where comets, meteors, and asteroids roam — without leaving Earth. Here are some museums and centres where you can find many different kinds of space exhibits.

The Science Museum
London

The London Planetarium
London

The Royal Observatory
Edinburgh, Scotland

The Exploratorium
Bristol, Avon

The Royal Greenwich Oservatory
Herstmonceux Castle, Hailsham, Sussex

Armagh Planetarium
Armagh, Northern Ireland

Dinosaurs and Other Prehistoric Animals
Exhibits of dinosaurs and other prehistoric animals are all over the world. Here are some places where you can see them in the United Kingdom.

Natural History Museum
London

Birmingham Museum
Birmingham, West Midlands

The Dinosaur Museum
Dorchester, Dorset

Hunterian Museum
Glasgow, Scotland

The University Museum
Oxford

Royal Scottish Museum
Edinburgh, Scotland

Museum of Isle of Wight Geology
Sandown, Isle of Wight

For More Information About Comets and the Dinosaurs

Here are some places you can write to for more information about space and prehistoric animals. Be sure to tell them exactly what you want to know about, and include your full name and address so they can write back to you.

Comets and Other Cosmic Treats

National Space Society
600 Maryland Avenue, SW
Washington, DC 20024, USA

The Planetary Society
65 North Catalina
Pasadena, California 91106, USA

Dinosaurs and Other Prehistoric Animals

Field Museum of Natural History
Roosevelt Road at Lake Shore Drive
Chicago, Illinois 60605, USA

Royal Ontario Museum
100 Queen's Park
Toronto, Ontario M5S 2C6, Canada

The University of Kansas
Museum of Natural History
Lawrence, Kansas 66045, USA

Glossary

asteroids: objects in space made of rock or metal that orbit the Sun mainly between Mars and Jupiter. An asteroid can be from one to several hundred miles in diameter.

colony: a group of people settled in a place away from their original home.

comet: an object made of ice, rock, and gas; has a vapour tail that may be seen when its orbit brings it close to the Sun.

crater: a hole in the ground caused by the impact of a meteorite striking Earth.

evolve: to develop or change over a long period of time.

galaxy: a huge group of stars and their satellites, as well as gas and dust. A galaxy might have tens of billions of stars. The Milky Way is our Galaxy.

gravity: the force that causes objects like the Earth and Moon to be attracted to one another.

iridium: a rare element that occurs more in extraterrestrial objects than in Earth's crust.

meteor: a meteoroid that has entered the Earth's atmosphere.

meteorite: a meteoroid when it hits Earth.

meteoroid: a lump of rock or metal drifting through space. Meteoroids can be as big as asteroids or as small as specks of dust.

Solar system: the Sun with the planets and all other bodies that orbit the Sun.

vaporize: to turn something that is liquid or solid into a gas.

Index

The publishers wish to thank the following for permission to reproduce copyright material: front cover, pp. 10-11, 13 (series of four), 16-17, © Julian Baum; pp. 4-5, 28-29, by Rudolf Zallinger, Peabody Museum of Natural History; p. 6, © Diane Gabriel, Milwaukee Public Museum; p. 7, Terry Huseby, © Discover Magazine (March, 1986); p. 8, © Allan E. Morton; p. 9 (both), Georg Gerster, Science Source; pp. 12-13, 14, 18-19, 20-21, © Mark Paternostro; p. 15, Leonid Kulik, courtesy of Smithsonian Institution; pp. 22-23, courtesy of European Southern Observatory; pp. 24-25, © Michael Carroll; pp. 26-27 (all), courtesy of NASA.

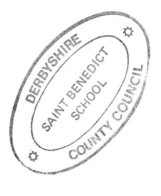